MAIN LIBRARY
ALBANY PUBLIC LIBRARY

DEC 0 5 2011

D1161995

MAIN LIBRARY
CARTHAGE PUBLIC LIBRARY

COPING WITH
DOMESTIC
VIOLENCE

Liz Miles

Heinemann
LIBRARY

Chicago, Illinois

www.heinemannraintree.com
Visit our website to find out
more information about
Heinemann-Raintree books.

To order:
☎ Phone 888-454-2279
🖥 Visit www.heinemannraintree.com
to browse our catalog and order online.

© 2011 Heinemann Library
an imprint of Capstone Global Library, LLC
Chicago, Illinois

All rights reserved. No part of this publication
may be reproduced or transmitted in any form or
by any means, electronic or mechanical, including
photocopying, recording, taping, or any information
storage and retrieval system, without permission in
writing from the publisher.

Edited by Louise Galpine and Laura Knowles
Designed by Richard Parker
Picture research by Liz Alexander

Originated by Capstone Global Library Ltd
Printed and bound in the United States of America,
North Mankato, MN

15 14 13 12 11
10 9 8 7 6 5 4 3 2 1

Library of Congress Cataloging-in-Publication Data
Miles, Liz.
Coping with domestic violence / Liz Miles.
p. cm. — (Real life issues)
Includes bibliographical references and index.
ISBN 978-1-4329-4762-0 (hc)
1. Family violence. I. Title.
HV6626.M534 2011
362.82'92—dc22
2010021046

Acknowledgments
The author and publisher are grateful to the following
for permission to reproduce copyright material:
© Capstone Publishers p. 30 (Karon Dubke); Alamy
pp. 10 (© www.Beepstock.com/Robinbeckham), **12**
(© Picture Partners), 18 (© Martyn Vickery), **21**
(© Chris Rout), 25 (© Hatonthestove), 26 (© Gabe
Palmer), 28 (© UK Stock Images Ltd), 34 (© Angela
Hampton Picture Library), **15** (© Richard Church),
43 (© MBI), Corbis pp. 11 (© Gerard Launet/
PhotoAlto), **16** (© Roy Morsch), 22 (© Ghislain &
Marie David de Lossy/cultura); Getty Images pp. **23**
(Jason Merritt), 27 (Steven Puetzer/Photographer's
Choice), **29** (Hill Street Studios/Blend Images), 37
(Andy Lee/First Light), 39 (Priscilla Coleman), **41**
(David Perez Shadi/Taxi); Photolibrary pp. **4**
(Enrique Algarra/age fotostock), 5 (Dave L. Ryan/
Index Stock Imagery), **33** (Cade Martin/
Uppercut Images), 35 (Radius Images); Press
Association Images p. 38 (Siddharth Darshan
Kumar/AP); Rex Features p. 9 (BURGER/Phanie);
Science Photo Library p. 14 (DR. P. MARAZZI);
Shutterstock p. 6 (© ejwhite).

"Distressed texture" design detail reproduced with
permission of iStockphoto/© Diana Walters.

Cover photograph of a girl reproduced with
permission of iStockphoto/© Shelly Perry.

Extracts on pages 8, 24, 32 and 36 are from Audrey
Mullender et al., *Children's, Perspectives on Domestic
Violence* (Thousand Oaks, Calif.: Sage, 2002).

We would like to thank Anne Pezalla for her
invaluable help in the preparation of this book.

Every effort has been made to contact copyright
holders of material reproduced in this book. Any
omissions will be rectified in subsequent printings if
notice is given to the publishers.

In order to protect the privacy of individuals, some
names in this book have been changed.

Disclaimer
All the Internet addresses (URLs) given in this book
were valid at the time of going to press. However,
due to the dynamic nature of the Internet, some
addresses may have changed, or sites may have
changed or ceased to exist since publication. While
the author and publisher regret any inconvenience
this may cause readers, no responsibility for any
such changes can be accepted by either the author
or the publisher.

CONTENTS

Stay safe on the Internet!
When you are on the Internet, never give personal details such as your real name, phone number, or address to anyone you have only had contact with online. If you are contacted by anyone who makes you feel uncomfortable or upset, don't reply, tell an adult, and block that person from contacting you again.

Any words appearing in the text in bold, **like this**, are explained in the glossary.

Introduction

Domestic violence is when family members or people in a relationship repeatedly treat each other very badly. The **abuse** can be **physical** (such as hitting) or **emotional** (such as calling you names to upset you). Both types of abuse are hurtful. Because of the different types of domestic violence, the term "domestic abuse" is sometimes used instead of "domestic violence."

Where?

Domestic violence takes place in the family home or in places the family visits. Often, no one else knows it is going on. It is kept a secret.

Abuse can be physical, verbal, or emotional, but no type of abuse is ever acceptable.

Who?

Domestic violence can happen between adults, such as a mother and father, or between younger people, such as brothers and sisters. It may also involve an adult or even an older brother or sister being violent to children. Violence toward children is called **child abuse**. Domestic violence tends to happen mostly between men and women, with the man being violent toward the woman. However, women abuse men sometimes, too.

Say "No!"

Abuse causes all kinds of feelings in the **victim**, such as sadness, fear, and anger. It is important for people to get help if they are experiencing abuse or violence. Nobody should have to accept being abused. This book will explain how and where to get help.

Domestic violence can continue for many years in a family home.

Your Rights

Domestic violence is wrong. There is no excuse for **abuse**, and the **victim** is never responsible. It should never happen, yet it does happen all around the world.

Everyone has the right to be treated with respect. There is no excuse for domestic violence.

Online!

Every human being has a right to be respected and treated well. International laws and agreements protect human rights. An abuser is not respecting the rights of his or her **victim**. You can find out about your rights by viewing the Convention on the Rights of the Child online (see page 47).

Children's rights

Children have the right to be looked after by the adults who care for them. The adults' duty is called their parental responsibility. If parents or caregivers **neglect** or treat children badly, they can be taken to **court**. Just as violence toward children is a form of abuse, so is neglect.

Is it a crime?

There is no single **criminal offense** covering domestic violence. This is because there are many different types of abuse. However, many of the things that **abusers** do are crimes. For example, making people frightened of violence is a crime, as is an actual **assault** causing harm. If you are being abused, it helps to remember that the law is there to help you.

BEHIND THE HEADLINES

The charity UNICEF tries to protect children. For example, in its 2010 Humanitarian Action report it said it needed almost $37 million for child protection around the world. This included money to help governments prevent **child abuse** in their countries.

There are many different forms of domestic violence. Most have to do with one person having power over another. The **abuser** hurts the **victim** in some way, making the person feel miserable, worthless, and powerless. By making the victim feel weak, the abuser feels that he or she can gain more control.

Verbal abuse

Shouting is a form of **verbal abuse**. Verbal abuse can control, mock, embarrass, threaten, and upset the victim. If someone shouts at you, it is shocking and can make you feel angry and upset. Constant yelling, threats, and swearing are frightening. You may fear you will be **physically** harmed next. Don't put up with verbal abuse from abusers—tell them to stop and ask them to apologize.

Abusers can use criticism to hurt their victims. This might include telling them they are useless or embarrassing them in front of other people. Not talking or replying to someone is also a form of verbal abuse. To be left out and ignored can be as hurtful as being shouted at.

CASE STUDY

Constant shouting is often a part of threatening behavior. A 16-year-old girl remembers the shouting that came with abuse: "It was the worst part of my life—constantly being shouted at, frightened, living in fear. You will never know what it was like, thinking that every day could be your last." An 8-year-old girl remembers threats: "He used to say, 'I am going to kill you at night-time when you are asleep.' … I used to get very frightened." Some children are unwilling to talk about their experiences so publicly.

An abuser may use verbal threats. This is unacceptable behavior.

Emotional abuse

You may feel you are being abused, even though the abuser is not actually saying anything abusive or hitting you. There are many forms of abuse that are not obvious, but that can affect your emotions.

Control

Controlling other people's lives is a form of **emotional** abuse. A husband in the family might take control of all the money, so no one else can make decisions about what to buy. A mother may have to ask for money just to buy food. She might have to explain every penny she has spent. The abuser might insist on making *all* the family decisions. This is abusive and unfair. Family decisions should be discussed. If you feel that someone is too controlling in your home, talk to an adult you trust.

Abused children often feel alone.

Isolation

Some abusers **isolate** their victims so that it is harder for them to get help. They might stop the victim from seeing friends or relatives from using the telephone, and shut the victim up in the house.

CASE STUDY

Imprisonment is an extreme case of control. In 2010 a 14-year-old U.S. girl was locked in her bathroom for nearly two months by her father. She had to sleep on a blanket and was given very little to eat. Luckily, she escaped through the attic and raced off on her bike. She went to a coffee shop, where an adult called the police. Her father and stepmother were arrested for **child abuse**, kidnapping, and **unlawful imprisonment**. The brave girl is now safe.

Special **helplines** offer advice to victims of all kinds of abuse and can help you feel less isolated.

Hearing violence between parents, such as shouting and screaming and plates crashing, is very frightening. If you witness violence like this, try to talk about it with an adult you can trust.

Physical abuse

Physical violence involves a person physically hurting another person, such as pushing, hitting, punching, kicking, or pinching someone. It can also involve throwing objects. Thousands of children **witness** physical violence or are a victim of it. Many people and organizations are trying to stop it. If you witness violence, don't risk getting involved by trying to stop it yourself. Instead, get help from an adult or by calling the police.

CASE STUDY

A 10-year-old girl had to leave home with her mother to escape from domestic violence. Her father was hitting her mother every day. They were glad to get away, yet it seemed unfair that they had to leave their home, when it was the father who was the violent one.

Child sexual abuse

Sexual abuse is when someone makes you feel uncomfortable by touching or looking at you in ways that are overly personal or rude. A sexual abuser can also make you feel uncomfortable in other ways, too, such as by showing you private parts of his or her body. If this happens to you, you should tell an adult you trust. It is wrong. It is not your fault and it should be stopped.

Crossing the Line

Sometimes children are not sure whether they are being **abused** or not, or whether what is happening to them is normal or wrong. **Abusers** may tell their children that the abuse is a punishment, and that they deserve it because they have misbehaved. However, it is important to remember that no one has the right to hurt you or to make you feel scared. All forms of abuse are wrong, and there is never any excuse.

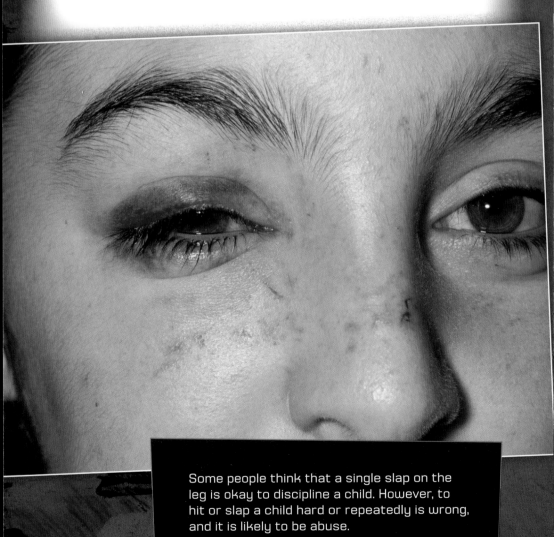

Some people think that a single slap on the leg is okay to discipline a child. However, to hit or slap a child hard or repeatedly is wrong, and it is likely to be abuse.

False reports

It is unfair to report domestic violence to the police if it is not happening. But if you are worried about how you are being treated and you are not sure if it is abuse or not, you must talk to an adult you trust, such as your teacher. It is important to tell someone how you feel.

Parents must teach their children right from wrong. They have the right to discipline their children for bad behavior. But they do not have the right to hurt them.

Online!

Abusers can use cell phones to control their **victims** or to abuse them in other ways. To find out more, go to the Safe Space website (see page 47). If someone is using your cell phone to abuse or control you, look at the list of suggestions for what you can do.

Cell phones help you keep in touch and stay safe, but they can also be used by abusers to control their victims.

Teen violence

Domestic violence between young people is thought to be increasing. In the United States, 33 percent of teenage girls are victims of **physical**, **emotional**, or **verbal** abuse from a dating partner. Too many young people do not understand how wrong this behavior is.

Research shows that some teenage boys are violent toward the girls they are dating. **Helplines** offer advice and support to the victims.

BEHIND THE HEADLINES

In March 2003, a case of teenage dating violence made national headlines. Sixteen-year-old Marcus McTear, a popular football star in Austin, Texas, stabbed his 15-year-old ex-girlfriend, Ortralla Mosley, to death in the school hallway. The couple had at first seemed like a perfect couple. But the longer they dated, Marcus became more controlling and violent with Otralla. Shortly before the stabbing, Otralla had broken up with Marcus, which enraged him. The tragedy of Otralla's murder served as a reminder that early signs of controlling and violent behavior in teenage relationships should be taken very seriously.

Awareness

In 2010 the U.S. Senate decided to extend a Teen Dating Violence Awareness and Prevention Week into a National Teen Dating Violence Awareness and Prevention Month. This will take place every February and help spread the message that violence is never okay. The decision to have an awareness month was made after research showed the increasing dangers of domestic violence faced by teenage girls in the United States.

Making parents and schools more aware of the violence between dating teens is important. If people don't know violence is happening, how can they help? It also helps to educate people that they are not to blame for their abuse. If you are worried that a teenager is a victim of violence, talk to an adult you can trust.

Violence toward women

Some women are violent toward men, but most domestic violence involves men attacking women. A study in the United States showed that 92 percent of victims of ongoing domestic violence between adults were women. Unfortunately, some people think that violence toward women is not as bad as it is. Many people do not understand that the victims need help.

If your mom is being abused, give her lots of love and try to encourage her to get help. Sometimes she may not be able to think clearly because she is so upset.

If you **witness** violence between your parents or caregivers, talk to an adult or call a helpline. It is upsetting to see and you will need support.

Myths

Here are some myths about violence against women:

- "Some women deserve it."
  WRONG: No one deserves to be abused. All forms of domestic abuse are bad.

- "It's not his fault he is violent—he just can't control his temper."
  WRONG: A loss of temper is no excuse. Anger is a natural feeling, but violence is not an acceptable way of showing your feelings.

- "Emotional abuse isn't domestic violence."
  WRONG: Just like being hit, emotional abuse hurts the victim and is dangerous and damaging.

WHAT DO YOU THINK?

When the Australian government ran a campaign called "Violence against women: Australia says no," a few people argued that it was unfair to focus the campaign on men being violent toward women. What do you think? Does the focus of the campaign sound like a good idea?

The campaign was fair	The campaign was unfair
The majority of domestic violence is carried out by men toward women.	Men are victims of domestic violence, too. Campaigns should be against all domestic violence.
Domestic violence is a serious issue. Any campaign that raises awareness of the problem is a good thing.	Some men might not report being victims of domestic violence because they feel embarrassed or think people won't believe them. Campaigns like this one don't help.

Fears and Worries

It is very upsetting to see someone being **abused** in your home. If you **witness** domestic abuse, you probably feel all kinds of emotions, such as fear, anger, and loneliness. All these feelings are natural. However, it is important to remember that the abuse is not your fault, and that it can be stopped.

Children's advice

It helps to know how other children have coped. Many children who have experienced domestic violence have good advice to give. For example, one group suggested that it is important to stay calm and think things through. Once you are calm, it is easier to decide what to do to solve the problem.

Online!

When facing violence in your life, understanding your own feelings is important. Looking on the Internet for advice can help, too. For example, the Childhelp website reminds you of important points, such as the fact that any abuse is not your fault and that hitting is against the law. It explains that it is best not to try to stop any violence yourself or to protect someone, or you could get hurt. If you witness violence, it is best to get help. See pages 46 and 47 for websites that can provide useful advice about dealing with domestic violence.

Worries at home can make you feel unwell. Some children cannot sleep, while others might get a stomachache. Feeling like this means it is time to get help.

Common worries

Sometimes children are **physically** attacked by their mother or father or by another relative. Sometimes the abuse might take another form. Whatever type of abuse it is, it can feel terrifying to the **victim**. It causes all sorts of worries and problems.

Children often worry that being abused is their own fault. This is not true. It is always the **abuser's** fault, not the child's. Children also worry that they will be made to feel embarrassed if they say anything. In fact, abuse is only embarrassing for the abuser. Children should never feel ashamed and should always tell someone if they are being abused. It is hard to tell someone that the person you love, or once loved, is hurting you. But whoever the abuser is, the abuse must be stopped.

Telling someone about abuse often brings a feeling of great relief.

Rihanna was abused by her boyfriend. Her story was in many newspapers, so it made people more aware of how victims feel.

CASE STUDY

Victims of violence often feel alone, as if they are the only person being abused. Singer Rihanna was interviewed about her ex-boyfriend attacking her. She explained how it can happen to anyone. She also reminded us that abuse is not the victim's fault. She said, "This happened to me. I didn't cause this. I didn't do it."

Love and hate

It is confusing when the abuser is someone the child loves, such as his or her father. However, no matter how much the child cares for the abuser, the kindest thing to do is to get help. Stopping the abuse is good for both the victim and the abuser. Calling a **helpline** is a useful first step.

Steps to Safety

There are many ways to stop the cycle of domestic violence in a home. Every year thousands of families receive help and the **abuse** stops.

It isn't always easy to leave

Victims might find it difficult to take steps to get help or to escape their **abuser**. Some of the reasons are:

- fear of being attacked if they leave
- feeling it's their fault and having low **self-esteem**
- worries about money and how they will support themselves and their families alone
- not having friends or knowing where to go for help.

If you know someone who is being abused, you can help support that person by encouraging him or her to tell other adults about the abuse.

CASE STUDY

During a group interview, children explained: "Grown-ups think they should hide it and shouldn't tell us, but we want to know. We want our moms … to talk to us about what they are going to do—we could help make decisions."

Many abused people feel too ashamed to get help. It is the abuser's fault that they feel like this.

What to do

If you **witness** abuse at home, you can start to find a way out by following this advice:

- Tell someone about the abuse. If possible, talk to the person being hurt.
- Talk to a teacher, neighbor, friend, or friend's parent. Choose someone you can trust.
- If you want to get advice without anyone knowing, you can contact a professional through a telephone **helpline** or the Internet.

Whom to tell?

Whether you are a witness to domestic violence or a victim, there are many professional, caring people to talk to. You might prefer to talk to another family member or a teacher. Thousands of children call helplines. Some call the police. However, you might prefer to get advice on the Internet. Always ask an adult to help you if you contact people on the Internet.

Sharing your worries with a trusted person, such as a teacher, means that you do not need to cope on your own anymore.

Help on the Internet

You might choose to visit a website to read the stories of other people in the same situation. The Childhelp website has a section where children write about their experiences. Sometimes it can be very helpful to know that you are not alone, and that other young people have struggled with the exact same experiences that you are now dealing with.

If you do not want to speak on a telephone, you can email many organizations, such as Childhelp, for advice.

Online!

You might be worried that the abuser will discover you are seeking help or talking about the abuse on your computer. However, nearly all websites that offer help on domestic violence give you instructions on covering your tracks. For example, the National Domestic Violence website provides a "quick escape" button, in case you abuser comes into the room. Abusers can become very angry if they know you are seeking help, so the instructions are worth following.

Helplines

Toll-free number helplines such as Childhelp offer advice on domestic violence and other problems. This helpline has handled more than two million calls since it was set up in 1982.

The **counselors** who answer helplines are specially trained to help you. They will not judge you and will not be shocked by anything you say. Most helplines promise to keep everything you say **confidential**, which means they will not pass on anything you have said to anyone else. You can choose to be **anonymous**, meaning you do not have to give your name.

Specially trained counselors answer calls to helplines such as Childhelp.

If someone is being attacked at home, children often choose to call the police.

In an emergency

Even if you need to stop an attack in your home, you must stay safe yourself. It is not your responsibility to step in or risk getting hurt. In an emergency, if you can't get help from an adult such as a neighbor, call 911 and ask for the police. They will come quickly to help, at any time of day or night. They will make sure you are safe.

CASE STUDY

Gracie's stepfather was often violent toward her mother. One day her stepfather slapped her mother so hard across the face that she fell on the floor. Her mother shouted to Gracie to run and call the police. Gracie ran next door, called the police, and explained about the fight. The police had been to the house before. They came right away and arrested Gracie's stepfather.

Safe and Cared For

It is often hard to leave an **abuser**, but sometimes it is the best thing to do. Adults may decide to escape from their abuser by:

- leaving home. This might be just for a while or forever.
- getting the abuser to leave
- taking legal action against the abuser. This means using the law to force the abuser to stay away or to arrest the abuser.

Sometimes women feel so threatened by an abuser that they do not dare to go back home. They may be worried about the safety of their children, too.

Getting away

If it is too dangerous to stay at home, a child or children and their mother may go to stay with relatives or friends, or go to a **shelter**. A family may have to take very few things with them and leave in a hurry before the abuser notices. If you think you might have to rush away suddenly with a parent, pack a small bag and hide it in a safe place. Include a favorite toy, such as a soft animal to cuddle.

Restraining orders

In some cases of **abuse**, people go to **court** to get a **restraining order** against an abuser. This means that the abuser is not allowed to get near the person (or people) he or she abused. The abuser might also be prevented from making any kind of contact, such as emails or letters. If the abuser does not obey the restraining order, he or she can be arrested.

WHAT DO YOU THINK?

Many children are upset that they must leave home to get away from an abusive relative. They may have to move to another part of the country and start a new school. Do you think this is the right thing to happen?

Yes, the victim should move	No, the victim should stay
Moving away can be very upsetting, but it is the safest thing to do.	It is not fair that the **victim** has to move. The abuser should be made to move instead.
If the victim moves away somewhere secret, the abuser will not know where he or she is. The victim can live without fear.	The abuser should be arrested and sent to prison or be forced by law to stay away.

Where to go?

The safety and happiness of children is the most important issue in cases of domestic abuse. Getting away from the abuser is often the first, most important step. This may mean going to:

- a shelter
- a relative or friend's house
- a **children's home** or **foster home**.

Children may need to go to a children's home or foster home for a while if there is not a parent, relative, or other caregiver to look after them.

What is a shelter?

A shelter is a safe, secret house or building to escape to. Several mothers and children live in a shelter, and people who work at the shelter take care of them. These workers might organize trips for the children and teenagers, such as to a movie theater or shopping center. However, sometimes the mothers or children are too nervous to go outside, in case the abuser finds them.

CASE STUDY

Children might feel sad to leave home and go to a shelter or move to another area. However, for many the feeling of safety outweighs the sadness. Here are some comments from children who have escaped from domestic violence:

"I feel safe now because I know no one can come and harm us." (9-year-old girl)

"Things couldn't be better. I'm not seeing all the things I used to see that I didn't want to. I hated seeing those things. And I'm seeing Mom being happy instead, and laughing." (16-year-old boy)

Children affected by domestic abuse may go to live for a while with other relatives, such as their grandparents.

Taken into foster care

If your parents are cruel to you or **neglect** you, they may be sent to court. The court has the power to take you to live with people who can take better care of you. The court may decide you should live with foster parents or in a children's home.

A new life

A parent and his or her children may need to start a new life far away from the abuser. The children will have to go to a new school. These changes are worth it in the end, because they will help the family to be safe. The parent and children might all talk to a **counselor**, who can help them cope better with painful memories of the abuse.

Talking to a trained counselor helps children to start a new, happy life.

CASE STUDY

Toby, age 10, had to move with his mother to get away from his dad. He felt much happier without his father around, and his mother smiled a lot more, too. Toby felt freer—he could relax at last and be himself. He felt safe knowing that if his dad found them, they could call for help. His mother had a restraining order against his father, so his father would be arrested if he tried to get near them.

What will happen to the abuser?

Group programs or classes are run to help abusers. Trained group workers encourage the abusers to talk through their feelings. The abusers learn how to notice when they are becoming abusive and how to stop themselves. When possible, ex-abusers may be reunited with their family or be able to see their children again.

Free from domestic violence, a family can rebuild their lives.

Why Does It Happen?

If a parent, caregiver, or older relative is hurting you, then remember that you are not to blame. It is not your fault. Many **victims** believe they have caused the problems that led to the domestic violence, but they have not.

Abusers are often driven by a wish to have power and control. Other things can contribute to abusive behavior, but do not cause it by themselves. Some of these things are:

- alcohol
- drugs
- unemployment
- stress
- health problems
- past experiences, such as being **abused** themselves.

All of these problems can be solved with determination and help, such as counseling. Most people can cope with these problems without becoming an abuser.

CASE STUDY

An abuser will often blame the victim for what is happening, but there is never any excuse for being violent. This 12-year-old boy's dad tried to blame his mom. He remembers how this made him feel confused: "I don't know [whose fault it was]. My dad used to say it was my mom's. I don't know why, but I believed him, and then I didn't know who to believe.... I didn't know who to choose. But I think it was my dad's fault really." It is confusing when both parents blame each other for violence. But remember what abuse is and it will become clear which parent is the abuser. Keeping this clear in your mind will help you cope.

Alcohol and other problems can influence people's behavior. Alcohol can make people more aggressive.

Forced marriages

In some cultures, parents arrange a marriage, matching their child with a partner. If the marriage is against the will of one or both people, it is a forced marriage. Forced marriages are seen as a form of abuse by many governments and by the **United Nations**.

Children are sometimes forced to return to their parents' native country to marry. If you are frightened of being forced into a marriage, talk to a teacher at school or call a **helpline**.

Some people believe that children can get married at the age of 12. This is illegal in Western countries, where 18 (or 16 with parents' agreement) is the most common legal age.

Repeating patterns?

Why do certain people become abusers? In some cases, it may be connected to with the abuser's need to control other people. Other times the abuser is repeating an experience he or she had as a child. Most adults who are abusive were abused themselves as children. However, most children who are abused do not grow up to be abusive adults. Counseling helps children who have experienced domestic abuse to go on to live very happy lives.

BEHIND THE HEADLINES

In 2010 two brothers, ages 10 and 11, from Edlington, in England, were imprisoned for brutally torturing two young children, nearly killing one of them. The brothers had **witnessed** domestic abuse, and one brother was shown violent videos from an early age. A lawyer described their family life as "toxic." However, the judge decided that the boys had to be kept away from society because of their dangerous behavior.

This picture was drawn during the Edlington brothers' **court** case. The boys' faces were not drawn, to protect their identities.

Brave first step

Domestic violence is a terrible experience—whether you are a witness or the victim. But as we have seen, there are ways of coping, and there are many caring people who want to help you. Reaching out for help becomes easier after the first step has been made. The first brave phone call to a helpline or a talk with an adult you trust can change everything. Remembering that many other children have experienced the same thing helps, too. Reading their stories on websites such as Childhelp (see page 46) can be **inspiring** and comforting.

Awareness

It can take time to move away from domestic violence. Everyone in the home has to be aware of what is going on. The victims and witnesses must understand that it is not their fault, and that they should get help.

Rebuilding lives

Once a family or children have escaped from abuse, they can rebuild their lives. It can take time to cope with the past. Children sometimes find it helpful to paint pictures or write about what happened to them. Talking about feelings and supporting your family will make you all feel happier. Don't forget to give a few hugs to those you love.

Online!

Look through some of the recommended contacts on pages 46–47. If possible, ask a trusted adult to help you research domestic violence using the websites listed. Knowing and understanding more about domestic violence makes it easier to cope with it.

After escaping from domestic violence, a parent might find a new, kind partner with whom everyone feels safe.

Top Ten Tips for Coping with Domestic Violence

Dealing with domestic violence is often difficult, but you can overcome **abuse**. Here are some tips to help you cope as you look toward a new life:

1. Remember that there is no excuse for domestic violence. It should never happen. No matter what an **abuser** might say, it is wrong.

2. After experiencing abuse, find a quiet, safe place where you can calm down and think carefully about what to do.

3. Remember that domestic violence is never your fault.

4. Talk to an adult you can trust, such as a parent, other relative, teacher, neighbor, or friend of your parents. Tell them what is happening. They should support you and be there when you need them. They will help you get practical help, too, and more information about what to do.

5. Call a **helpline** (see pages 46–47). The people who answer will be caring and sensitive. They will have the knowledge and experience to be able to help you.

6. In an emergency, call 911 and ask for the police, or ask an adult to call them for you.

7. If you are planning to run away, call a helpline first, such as the National Runaway Switchboard.

8. Look at websites like Childhelp for advice and information. You can get personal advice by emailing or calling the websites (see pages 46–47 for the addresses).

9. If you are feeling angry, upset, or unhappy, try some of these ideas: write in a diary, find an empty space such as a field and scream, cry, draw a picture, call a friend, or talk to an adult you can trust. Remember that it is okay to feel strong emotions.

10. Always remember that help is waiting for you. You can find **confidential** help on the telephone any time, day or night.

Writing about your feelings in a diary can help you to figure things out. If you later read through what you have written, you might be able to come up with solutions to any problems.

Glossary

abuse harm or cruelty

abuser person who harms or hurts someone repeatedly

anonymous no telling anyone your name. If you choose to remain anonymous, no one knows it is you talking.

assault illegal attack on someone, which may harm the victim

child abuse harm that is done repeatedly to a child, ranging from neglect to hitting

children's home home for children whose parents are unable to look after them. Children may stay in a children's home for a short time while waiting to return to their parents or to be found a foster home.

confidential kept secret

counselor person who has been trained to give advice or to guide people as they make decisions and try to cope with life

court place where a judge makes legal decisions. People who have broken the law go to court for a trial.

criminal offense act that can be punished by law. Punching someone is a criminal offense.

emotional to do with feelings or emotions, and having strong feelings. Victims of abuse often feel emotional.

foster home family that offers a home to children who need one. Staying in a foster home is like living with a new family.

helpline telephone service offering advice

inspiring giving encouragement or new ideas

isolate keep someone away from other people so that he or she cannot see or talk to others

neglect lack of care. Child neglect can mean that a child is not given enough love, food, education, warmth, or safety.

physical to do with the body. If someone hits you, that is physical abuse.

restraining order legal order that prevents someone—often an abuser—to stay away from a person, and perhaps even to end any kind of communication at all

self-esteem person's belief in his or her own worth and abilities

sexual to do with sex, and the private parts of your body, or the private parts of another person's body

shelter safe place for abused women and children to escape to

toll-free number telephone number that does not cost anything to call

United Nations worldwide organization concerned with world peace, security, and human rights

unlawful imprisonment locking someone up against his or her will, which therefore breaks the law

verbal spoken or said. Verbal abuse involves shouting or saying words that hurt, upset, or frighten the listener.

victim person who is hurt by someone else.

witness person who sees or hears something happen

Find Out More

Books

Murphy, Patricia. *Divorce and Separation* (*Tough Topics*). Chicago: Heinemann Library, 2008.

Sanders, Pete. *Violent Feelings* (*Choices and Decisions*). Mankato, Minn.: Stargazer, 2006.

Stewart, Sheila. *When Daddy Hit Mommy* (*Kids Have Troubles Too*). Broomall, Pa.: Mason Crest, 2011.

Websites and organizations

The following websites and organizations can offer help and support to you and your family:

Childhelp
www.childhelp.org
Tel: 1-800-4-A-CHILD
Childhelp helps children who have been neglected or abused. There is a helpline where you can talk to counselors 24 hours a day, 7 days a week.

National Domestic Violence Hotline
www.thehotline.org
Tel: 1-800-799-SAFE
You can call this toll-free number for help 24 hours a day, 7 days a week. The organization's website has lots of information on domestic violence, including information about teen dating violence and stories about how people have coped with domestic violence.

Convention on the Rights of the Child
www.unicef.org.uk/tz/resources/assets/pdf/
    every_child_colour_leaflet.pdf
Find out about your rights in this leaflet made by UNICEF.

National Runaway Switchboard
www.nrscrisisline.org
Tel: 1-800-RUNAWAY
This is a free helpline you can call for help and advice if you are
thinking of running away, or have run away.

The Safe Space
www.thesafespace.org
You can look on this website for information and advice if you
are worried about dating violence, or if you feel like someone is
using a cell phone to control you.

Love Is Respect: National Teen Dating Abuse Hotline
www.loveisrespect.org
Tel: 1-866-331-9474
You can call a toll-free number or go to the website for a live chat
if you have worries about dating abuse.

National Association for Children of Alcoholics (Nacoa)
www.nacoa.org
Tel: 1-888-55-4COAS
The National Association for Children of Alcoholics can offer
advice and support if your parent has a drinking problem.

Index